CELEBRATING THE FAMILY NAME OF ALI

Celebrating the Family Name of Ali

Walter the Educator

Silent King Books
a WhichHead Entertainment Imprint

Copyright © 2024 by Walter the Educator

All rights reserved. No part of this book may be reproduced in any manner whatsoever without written permission except in the case of brief quotations embodied in critical articles and reviews.

First Printing, 2024

Disclaimer

This book is a literary work; the story is not about specific persons, locations, situations, and/or circumstances unless mentioned in a historical context. Any resemblance to real persons, locations, situations, and/or circumstances is coincidental. This book is for entertainment and informational purposes only. The author and publisher offer this information without warranties expressed or implied. No matter the grounds, neither the author nor the publisher will be accountable for any losses, injuries, or other damages caused by the reader's use of this book. The use of this book acknowledges an understanding and acceptance of this disclaimer.

Celebrating the Family Name of Ali is a memory book that belongs to the Celebrating Family Name Book Series by Walter the Educator. Collect them all and more books at WaltertheEducator.com

USE THE EXTRA SPACE TO DOCUMENT YOUR FAMILY MEMORIES THROUGHOUT THE YEARS

ALI

Ali, a name of strength and grace,

With roots that span both time and space.

A banner held through trials and strife,

A shining beacon of noble life.

From desert sands to bustling square,

The name Ali is whispered there.

A legacy forged in courage and might,

Guiding hearts through darkest night.

It speaks of wisdom, bold and true,

Of paths once walked, of skies once blue.

With every tale, a lesson told,

Ali's story shines like gold.

The crescent moon, the guiding star,

Ali's spirit travels far.

In every land, in every tongue,

Its melody is proudly sung.

Through deeds of honor, love, and care,

The name Ali grows everywhere.

A steadfast bond, a family strong,

A name that echoes in every song.

In the markets hum or mosque's soft call,

The name Ali stands tall through all.

A pillar firm, unbent by time,

A legacy deep, profound, sublime.

Through ink on scrolls and swords in hand,

Ali's wisdom shaped the land.

A guardian's heart, a scholar's mind,

In Ali's name, resolve you'll find.

The sun may set, the stars may fade,

But Ali's light will never degrade.

It shines in stories, old and new,

A name of honor, pure and true.

Ali, a thread in history's weave,

A name that hearts cannot deceive.

A name of faith, of hope, of pride,

Forever cherished, far and wide.

So raise the banner, sing the name,

Ali's spirit burns like flame.

A family rich with roots so deep,

Its legacy eternal, for all to keep.

ABOUT THE CREATOR

Walter the Educator is one of the pseudonyms for Walter Anderson. Formally educated in Chemistry, Business, and Education, he is an educator, an author, a diverse entrepreneur, and he is the son of a disabled war veteran. "Walter the Educator" shares his time between educating and creating. He holds interests and owns several creative projects that entertain, enlighten, enhance, and educate, hoping to inspire and motivate you. Follow, find new works, and stay up to date with Walter the Educator™

at WaltertheEducator.com

www.ingramcontent.com/pod-product-compliance
Lightning Source LLC
LaVergne TN
LVHW012051070526
838201LV00082B/3906